Let's Read About Pets

Kittens

by JoAnn Early Macken

Reading consultant: Susan Nations, M.Ed., author/literacy coach/consultant

Please visit our web site at: www.earlyliteracy.cc
For a free color catalog describing Weekly Reader® Early Learning Library's list of high-quality books, call 1-877-445-5824 (USA) or 1-800-387-3178 (Canada). Weekly Reader® Early Learning Library's fax: (414) 336-0164.

Library of Congress Cataloging-in-Publication Data

Macken, JoAnn Early, 1953-
Kittens / by JoAnn Early Macken.
p. cm. – (Let's read about pets)
Summary: A simple introduction to kittens and how to care for them.
Includes bibliographical references and index.
ISBN 0-8368-3799-1 (lib. bdg.)
ISBN 0-8368-3846-7 (softcover)
1. Kittens–Juvenile literature. [1. Cats. 2. Animals–Infancy. 3. Pets.] I. Title.
SF445.7.M24 2003
636.8'07–dc21 2003045053

First published in 2004 by
Weekly Reader® Early Learning Library
330 West Olive Street, Suite 100
Milwaukee, WI 53212 USA

Editorial: JoAnn Early Macken
Art direction: Tammy Gruenewald
Page layout: Katherine A. Goedheer

Printed in the United States of America

1 2 3 4 5 6 7 8 9 07 06 05 04 03

Note to Educators and Parents

Reading is such an exciting adventure for young children! They are beginning to integrate their oral language skills with written language. To encourage children along the path to early literacy, books must be colorful, engaging, and interesting; they should invite the young reader to explore both the print and the pictures.

Let's Read About Pets is a new series designed to help children learn about the joys and responsibilities of keeping a pet. In each book, young readers will learn interesting facts about the featured animal and how to care for it.

Each book is specially designed to support the young reader in the reading process. The familiar topics are appealing to young children and invite them to read – and re-read – again and again. The full-color photographs and enhanced text further support the student during the reading process.

In addition to serving as wonderful picture books in schools, libraries, homes, and other places where children learn to love reading, these books are specifically intended to be read within an instructional guided reading group. This small group setting allows beginning readers to work with a fluent adult model as they make meaning from the text. After children develop fluency with the text and content, the book can be read independently. Children and adults alike will find these books supportive, engaging, and fun!

– Susan Nations, M.Ed., author, literacy coach,
and consultant in literacy development

At first, newborn kittens cannot see or hear. When they are three months old, they can see and hear very well.

A newborn kitten drinks its mother's milk. Later, it can eat solid food. Kittens also need fresh water.

All kittens have blue eyes when they are born. A kitten's eyes may change color when it gets older.

A kitten's fur may be long or short. It may be white, black, orange, gray, or other colors. It may have stripes or spots.

Kittens lick their fur to keep it clean. You can brush your kitten's fur to keep it free from tangles.

A kitten's tail
is part of its
backbone. A
kitten uses its
tail to balance.

A kitten may mew or meow when it sees you. A kitten may purr when you hold it. An angry kitten might growl, hiss, or spit.

A kitten starts to play when it is about four weeks old. It may pounce on a toy or chase a ball.

After all that work, a kitten needs to rest! All kittens need a lot of sleep.

Glossary

pounce – to jump on something and grab it

purr – a low rumbling sound made by a happy cat

solid – not a gas or a liquid

tangles – snarls or knots

For More Information

Fiction Books

Root, Phyllis. *Here Comes Tabby Cat.*
Cambridge, Mass: Candlewick Press, 2000.

Tuxworth, Nicola. *Kittens: A Very First Picture Book.*
Milwaukee: Gareth Stevens, 1999.

Nonfiction Books

Meadows, Graham. *Cats.*
Milwaukee: Gareth Stevens, 1998.

Neye, Emily. *All About Cats and Kittens.*
New York: Grosset & Dunlap, 1999.

Web Sites

About Cats

www.cats.org.uk/htm/about_cats.htm

Cat facts, photos, and tips from Cats Protection

Index

About the Author

JoAnn Early Macken is the author of two rhyming picture books, *Sing-Along Song* and *Cats on Judy*, and three other series of nonfiction books. She teaches children to write poetry, and her poems have appeared in several children's magazines. A graduate of the M.F.A. in Writing for Children and Young Adults program at Vermont College, she lives in Wisconsin with her husband and their two sons.